Meditation Handbook for Beginners

by Nita Lapinski

©2013 Nita Lapinski

Introduction

Welcome to the world of meditation; I am honored to share this time with you. Like you, I am a student of meditation. This instruction is designed to be a six-week course, each meditation building on the one before it. The meditations should be practiced daily for a minimum of one week before moving on to the next. Keep a meditation journal to map your growth.

The techniques in this course stem from various philosophies that include teachings from Edgar Casey, Native American traditions, and East Indian philosophy, and have been taught by what I consider to be my best instructors—Mietek Wirkus,* Debbie Ford, and Kathleen Barratt.* Wirkus teaches bio-energy, and from him I learned about chakras and their emotional connection, as well as

Candle Gaze and Heart Meditation. A more in-depth instruction can be found in his student manual, *Bio-Energy: A Healing Art* by Margret Wirkus. Under Barratt I learned integrative breath work and meditation. These meditations and practices have been staples in my life, and I have practiced and taught them for years with great results.

We have been told for years, "clear your mind of all thoughts," or "meditate for a half hour to an hour a day." This is sage advice but not always practical in today's world. I found when learning meditation that clearing your mind is nearly impossible. Yet, with continued practice you will achieve a quieted mind but you must be patient. Allow yourself to learn. I teach my students to commit ten minutes a day to meditation. More is better, but if ten minutes is what you can fit in comfortably and stick to it, it will change your life. Do your best to follow the instruction in this guide. It's especially important when you're learning to create a habit of meditation that is practical for you and then stay with it. I had a student who meditated for five minutes three times a day and for him the practice brought a sense of calmness and a connection to his inner-voice. It also helped him overcome insomnia. Create a foundation and make the meditations and how you practice them your own.

*Margret & Mietek Wirkus Bio-Relax
www.mietekwirkus.com
*Kathleen Barratt
www.barrattbreathworks.com

"At the end of the day, I can end up just totally wacky, because I've made mountains out of molehills. With meditation, I can keep them as molehills."

Ringo Starr

Preparing For Meditation

Establishing a habit is very helpful when beginning a meditation practice. I recommend creating a specific place and time, and following the same format before each meditation. In this way we teach our brain to be ready to reach deeper states of relaxation. I use intent followed by prayer before every meditation. Choosing intent is important because it sets the direction of your meditation. Keep your intention simple. For example, my intent is to be in Christ, Buddha, God, Spirit, consciousness only, etc. I choose to follow intent with silent prayer.

- Begin your music, if you choose. I recommend *Spirit Wind* by Richard Warner.

- Find a comfortable position that allows you to keep your spine erect in order to ensure good energy flow. (I use a Rama chair available at zenbydesign.com)

- Take three deep and relaxing breaths. Fill your lungs to capacity and then slowly exhale.

- Tilt your head to the left—ear to shoulder—three times, and then to the right three times. Follow this with three head rolls to the left, and three to the right.

- Press your finger gently against the opening of your right nostril and inhale through the left. Exhale through both nostrils. Do this three times on the left side. Then switch and inhale through your right nostril, this time exhaling through your mouth; again three times.

- To bring your vibration higher, chant "OM" three times. Don't be shy. Let it rip.

- Finally, you are ready to silently speak your intention followed by prayer.

- Keep a meditation journal.

Energy Levels

"Chakra" means "spinning wheel" in Sanskrit, which is in the Indian yoga system, or "khorlo" in the Tibetan system. We will explore the basics of the chakra system in the etheric field of energy for this course through the practice of pulling energy up through the chakras and learning to balance the centers. There are several bodies of energy around us. Each has its own chakras system that links with our physical body and emotional body. As you advance in meditation, I recommend that you further study of the various fields of energy that surround and support the physical body.

"Remember what people used to say about meditation? Now everyone is doing it."

Shirley MacLaine

The Etheric, Thermal, or Electromagnetic Field

The field immediately surrounding the physical body is called the etheric, thermal, or electromagnetic field. This energy is the easiest to see and feel, and generally radiates two or three inches from the body. There are patterns in this field specific to each person, much like a vibrational thumbprint. The patterns can show lifestyle, fear, depression, sadness, drug use, loss, ADD, Autism, or the opposites of these, and even fluctuate when a person is dishonest. Fields vary with individuals depending on their general health and wellbeing. For example, if a person is sick or in pain, their field may be low and dull. Conversely, a bright, full field radiates when the same person is in good health or high spirits.

The color of fields varies from soft hues of pink, violet, blue, or silver, to browns and grays.

- All living organisms have an etheric field.

- Each part of the physical body is connected with its equivalent in the etheric body. There is an etheric liver, heart, etc. Some believe that the reason transplants fail is because the etheric body of the recipient is not in harmony with the etheric body donor.

- The most important function of the etheric body is to supply our physical body with vital energy. It transfers energy from universal fields of the cosmos and "feeds" this to individual fields of human beings. Energy transfer goes through the energy centers in the etheric field called "chakras."

- There are seven main chakras in the etheric field, and each has a link with specific organs in the body as well as specific glands and their function. For our purpose in this six-week meditation course, we will focus on the etheric body.

Chakras and Organs Influenced

1. **Root Chakra:** Male and female reproductive organs/sex glands.

2. **Spleen Chakra:** The spleen gland is the most important energy center in the etheric field level as it absorbs and distributes energy. It "feeds" the whole energy system.

3. **Solar Plexus Chakra:** Adrenal glands, liver, pancreas, gallbladder, kidneys, stomach, digestive system, and sympathetic nervous system.

4. **Heart Chakra:** Heart, thymus gland, (until age nine or ten or adolescence, entire chest area.)

5. **Throat Chakra:** Thyroid gland.

6. **Third eye Chakra:** Pituitary gland and hypothalamus gland.

7. **Crown Chakra:** Pinal gland, brain.

The most important chakra in the etheric field is the spleen. It distributes the energy to all chakras except the third eye. Spleen chakra can indicate the health of an individual.

All human beings are born with chakras, which fully open around age eight to eleven-years-old. Chakras can vibrate at incorrect rates or become congested, but they never actually close or shut down unless the body is dead.

Colors of the chakras in the etheric field can differ from the astral level. They are usually much less luminescent and are a mixture of different colors with a predominant hue.

Traditional teachings of chakras show specific colors, but in truth the chakras are a blend of color. Mietek teaches that the chakra looks like a bicycle wheel with many spokes turning at a very high speed. On each spoke is a color, but when the wheel is spinning we can't differentiate the colors.

Chakras turn clockwise; **never counter clockwise**. Energy through the system always flows upward, never down. Chakras, like all vibration, make sounds that are unique to each living thing.

"Meditation while walking has a long, noble history in ancient spiritual disciplines."

Andrew Weil

Candle Gazing

Place a lit candle on the floor or table. Get comfortable and again, keep your spine erect. Choose a mantra that you can repeat silently throughout the meditation. Keep it simple. For example, "God and I are one," or "I am at peace," or "I am one with the light," etc. Relax your eyes and close them halfway. Simply gaze into the flame while mentally repeating your mantra. Avoid blinking. The goal of the meditation is to maintain uninterrupted focus.

During the meditation you may experience some resistance. This can manifest through body discomfort, sudden itching, excessive eye watering, blinking repeatedly, or mental chatter. It is okay. Just resume your mantra and continue to gaze into the flame. Many students experience complete background blackness, see multiple flames, a disappearing flame, or a combination of these. Again, this is normal. For optimum benefits, begin practicing this meditation for ten minutes and increase to fifteen and ultimately twenty-five to thirty minutes if possible. Practice this meditation everyday for at least one week before moving on to the next. I consider Candle Gaze to be a meditation staple. When you're having trouble finding your center, Candle Gazing is always effective. Meditation is an ebb and flow; sometimes we find it easy, sometimes not. Stick with it and create a habit of at least ten minutes a day. Remember to write in your journal.

"I meditate.
Meditation helps me."

Rick Springfield

Heart Meditation

Begin by choosing someone that is easy to love. It can be a person or an animal. The key here is that you have no struggle or conflict with the person you choose. Once you have chosen, allow your body to relax. Focus on the center of your chest (heart chakra), and fill that area with the love that you feel for the person you have chosen. Let that love gather in your heart center and then send the love out to them. Allow the energy of love to flow from your heart. Remember this meditation is not about thinking the word "love" or visualizing love. It is about *feeling* love from the deepest place within your body and sending it out to that person or to the world.

During this meditation you may experience tightening, fluttering, tingling, pressure, warmth, joy, or sadness and pain. Any sensation is okay because it indicates movement of energy.

You may even cry, which may be a much-needed release.

Practice heart meditation for at least ten days. Start by meditating for twenty minutes and slowly expand to thirty before moving on to the next meditation practice. If that is not possible, a minimum of ten minutes is needed.

After you become comfortable with this meditation, you may choose to work with more difficult relationships. When you do this, bring the person in question into focus and find something positive about them while concentrating on unconditional love. Practice this often and you will notice a shift to a more positive energy within your feelings. Keep track of your progress in your meditation journal.

"The purpose of meditation is personal transformation."

Henepola Gunaratana

Be Still, Know God

Relax your body and focus on your breath. On your first inhale silently speak, "Be still." Exhale. Inhale and exhale again. Do not repeat the mantra on this breath cycle. Instead, allow yourself to feel the stillness. On your third breath cycle, as you inhale silently speak, "Know god." You can easily change the words, "know god" to know self, spirit, peace, etc. Choose what you are comfortable with. Again, do not repeat the mantra on the following cycle. Rather, feel your connection with god, or what you consider your highest source, as you breathe. Repeat these breath cycles and mantras for ten minutes, increasing to thirty.

Using mantra and breath will help move you into an altered state of awareness. I find this particular meditation very peaceful.

Chakra Meditation

The goal of this meditation is to heal the emotional issues connected with each chakra in the etheric field, and to bring balance to the centers. This is done by pulling energy up through each chakra beginning at the base of the spine, and completing by spiraling out of the crown chakra. It is helpful to repeat affirmations, which facilitate the release of any congestion associated with each center.

Sit with your spine erect and begin at the base chakra. Feel the energy gather there as you breathe. Focus on that center and repeat the affirmation that connects with the chakra. After a few moments, pull the energy up into the next center. If during the meditation you forget where you are, always go to the next highest chakra rather than below. You may experience warmth, tingling, or tightness and discomfort. Just breathe through it and move on. Here are some affirmation suggestions that correspond with each center:

Affirmations that help release emotional energy when balancing chakras.

1. **Root:** I release my sadness. I release my fear. I am safe.
2. **Spleen:** My future is safe and secure. I am always where I need to be.
3. **Solar Plexus**: I release judgment. I am what I aspire to be.
4. **Heart:** I give and receive unconditional love. My heart is filled with joy.
5. **Throat:** I am gentle. I am patient. I speak my truth with love.
6. **Third Eye:** I easily manifest my ideals. I am willing to see all things.
7. **Crown:** No affirmation here, simply spiral energy out and upward clockwise. Send energy to your highest source.

Enter your experience in your journal and see how you grow.

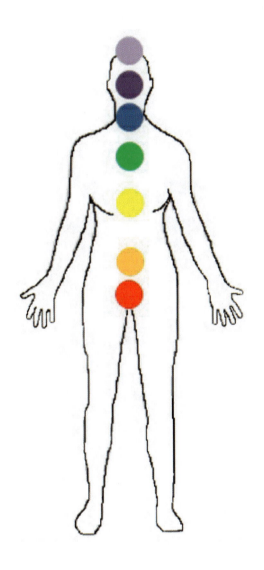

"What's encouraging about meditation is that even if we shut down, we can no longer shut down in ignorance. We see very clearly that we're closing off. That in itself begins to illuminate the darkness of ignorance."

Pema Chodron

Circle of Light

Using breath or "prana" to reach altered states of consciousness is very powerful. This modality should be used with respect. Relying on conscious connected breathing solely, without training or assistance, can catapult you into levels of awareness you may not wish to reach at this stage of your development. For this meditation we will control breathing in a count of cycles.

To start, become aware of energy, which begins in the base chakra. As you inhale, imagine this energy moving up the spine, rounding over the crown of your head, and pausing at Third Eye as you complete your inhale, having filled your lungs to capacity. As you exhale, allow the energy to shower from Third Eye over the front of your chakras, reconnecting in the base chakra and creating a circle of light. Do not pause after you exhale; begin your inhale immediately, repeating the first cycle. There is no pause between exhale and inhale. Continue with ten to fifteen cycles and then return to normal breathing. Conscious connected breathing can cause tetany, which is a tightening or cramping of the muscles. If this occurs at any point, return to your natural breathing cycle.

*You can find information on this meditation in the book, *The Secret of the Golden Flower: A Chinese Book of Life* (with a translation and explanation by Richard Wilhelm).

"Meditation is not a way of making your mind quiet. It's a way of entering into the quiet that's already there – buried under the 50,000 thoughts the average person thinks every day."

Deepak Chopra

The River

Another meditation that you might find helpful is one that relies on visualization. After your preparation, begin to visualize being part of a flowing river. Do your best to create a river that comes alive in your mind's eye. Create how the river sounds, and visualize its surroundings, such as the color of the sky, flowers, rocks, and trees near your river. Feel yourself actually flowing with the river, and then let yourself expand until you are the river. Stay with that for a few moments. Next, imagine yourself beginning to freeze. Visualize and feel what that might look like and feel like as you begin to thicken and slow. Allow yourself to become a solid freeze. Stay with how it feels to be frozen and still. When you're ready, begin to thaw. See and feel the thaw, allowing steam to rise up and up. This visualization can be repeated again and again during one session if you choose.

"Meditation is listening to the Divine within."

Edgar Cayce

Conscious Intent

We all experience fearful, negative thoughts, limiting beliefs, habitual behavior, and feelings of unworthiness. One way to shift these debilitating patterns is to use conscious intention. Though using conscious intention is not a meditation, it is a powerful practice that can shift anything we choose to focus on changing.

Practicing conscious thought, or intent, leads to a greater understanding of our experiences and ourselves, thus allowing us to heal. To use it is simple. First, choose your intent such as, releasing fear, judgment, anger, sadness, or criticism. Or you may choose to respond with love, acceptance, understanding, compassion, or grace.

The exercise can be done in five minutes, or you can incorporate it with meditation for longer periods. Find a comfortable place to sit or recline. Focus on breath as it fills your lungs to capacity, and then simply let it go. Notice your body relax with each exhale. Stay with your breath for several minutes. Bring your focus from your mind's eye to the center of your chest. Feel this area expand and open like a flower. You may feel fluttering, tingling, or tightening. You may even feel mild pain. Stay with your breath while you focus on the heart center. Feel love flow from your heart out into the world. Breathe that energy for a few moments.

Next, mentally speak your intent, "I release: fear, anger, resentment, sadness, etc.," or "I respond with: love, compassion, patience, understanding, etc." Repeat your intent as you breathe. Visualize a funnel of light that begins at your heart center and opens upward toward the heavens. Affirm your connection with god, spirit, or divine self. Breathe. When you're ready, close your hands and hold the energy within you. Know that you will carry your intention throughout the day. If during your day you forget to practice your intention, don't worry, simply reaffirm your intention mentally and anchor the thought in your heart.

About the Author

Nita Lapinski has been a working clairvoyant-medium for over three decades and offer's meditation classes and workshops on forgiveness, releasing judgment and finding one's intuition. She is a certified hypnotherapist and has studied integrative breath work and bio-energy. Both are modalities of healing emotional issues using breath and moving energy.

Nita resides in Arizona with her husband. She is also the author of *The Knowing-Awake in the Dark* available on Amazon. Visit her website at www.nitalapinski.com. You may also find her on *The Knowing* fan page at Facebook at http://www.facebook.com/bornintuition or email her at nitalapinski@gmail.com.

Made in the USA
Charleston, SC
30 August 2016